Red Under the Skin

1993 Agnes Lynch Starrett Poetry Prize

Red Under The Skin

Natasha Sajé

University of Pittsburgh Press
Pittsburgh • London

The publication of this book is supported by grants from the National Endowment for the Arts in Washington, D.C., a Federal agency, and the Pennsylvania Council on the Arts.

Published by the University of Pittsburgh Press, Pittsburgh, Pa. 15260

Library of Congress Cataloging-in-Publication Data

Sajé, Natasha.
 Red under the skin / Natasha Sajé.
  p.   cm. —(Pitt poetry series)
  ISBN 0-8229-3865-0 (alk. paper).—ISBN 0-8229-5545-8 (pbk.: alk. paper)
 I. Title.   II. Series.
 PS 3569.A45457R4 1994   94-21669
 811'.54—dc20   CIP

A CIP catalogue record for this book is available from the British Library.
Eurospan, London

The author and publisher wish to acknowledge the following publications in which some of these poems first appeared: *The American Voice* ("L'Oustau de Baumanière," "What I Want to Make for You"); *Antaeus* ("Chocolates," "Rampion"); *Chelsea* ("Reeling"); *Feminist Studies* ("Reading the Late Henry James," "Then What Is the Question?"); *Gettysburg Review* ("Edith Wharton After the Death of Henry James"); *Ploughshares* ("A Male in the Women's Locker Room," "Red Under the Skin," "What Difference Does It Make?"); *Poetry* ("A Short History of the Sybarites"); *Prairie Schooner* ("Tongues"); *Salmagundi* ("Appetites," "Salsify"); *Shenandoah* ("Eating Crabs with Bob and Jim," "'Game'"); *University of Windsor Review* ("Miss Cotton"); *Virginia Quarterly Review* ("Agoraphobia"); *Women's Review of Books* ("Dress Code," "In College, Linda"); and *Women's Studies* ("The Letter").

I am grateful to the friends who read and commented on drafts of my work, as well as to the Maryland State Arts Council, the Squaw Valley Community of Writers, and the University of Maryland English Department and the Office of Graduate Studies and Research for their support.

Paperback cover images and p.iii image are details from *Cherries, Pears and Butterfly,* a painting (right) by Stone Roberts.

Author photo: Leonard L. Greif, Jr.

Book Design: Frank Lehner

For my parents, Hiltrud and Josef Sajé

Contents

III.

IV. BODY LANGUAGE

Red Under the Skin

Reading the Late Henry James

is like having sex, tied to the bed.
Spread-eagled, you take whatever comes,
trusting him enough to expect
he'll be generous, take his time. Still
it's not exactly entertainment:
Page-long sentences strap
your ankles and chafe your wrists.
Phrases itch like swollen bee stings
or suspend you in the pause
between throbs of a migraine,
the pulsing blue haze
relieved. You writhe and twist—
if you were split in half,
could he get all the way in?
When you urge him to move faster,
skim a little,
get to the good parts, he scolds,
"It's all good parts."
Then you realize you're bound
for disappointment, and you begin
to extricate yourself,
reaching past his fleshy white fingers
for a pen of your own.

I. Ink

Creation Story

Vanilla
is the Emily Dickinson of orchids:
plain white flowers, yet its lush vine
can trail ten stories carried by the trees.
Green pods are cured dark walnut brown.
Sliced open lengthwise: infinitesimal seeds,
printer's ink. Their black flecks ice cream
or a sauce for pheasant or steeps in oil
where the scent lingers, like a morning moon.
The Aztecs used vanilla, brewed it salty for Columbus.
It took the English to make it sweet.
A cure for impotence, they thought,
smoking it with tobacco.
Cunt-struck, the Elizabethans said, when
drawn by a woman's scent
or the way she moved her head,
they wanted her more than words.
From the Spanish *vainilla,*
diminutive of Latin, *vagina,*
the term for *sheath.*
A vagina became a case—
a portico covering travelers,
a scabbard for a sword—
the way Ptolemy made the earth the center
and the Greeks named orchid tubers
after testicles.
No matter that some words glide over the tongue,
entice us with sweet stories,
we're still stuck
with their roots in our throats.

Baron Haussmann and the Plan of Paris

Let's give the city
stars, he said, looking at a map,
seeing the slender medieval alleys
named "old lantern" and "cold cloak,"
gabled half-timbered houses,
corner-turreted and spiral-staired hotels—
impediments to movement. Even the pointed roofs,
the severe and calm Renaissance order,
those too had to give way—
to seven-story apartments,
stone facades like pinstripes, gray.
At times he pondered the cost—
the demolished *quartiers,*
the poor banished to the city's frayed cuffs—
but without regret:
labyrinths breed cholera and crime,
structures are not sacred simply because they endure.
He ordered promenades from dumps, parks from gibbets,
sewers and drains where stagnant water once stood,
but he was proudest of the wide, sudden perspectives,
the broad avenues giving citizens
the sense of mountain climbers who,
after so long attending to their feet,
reach the top, take a breath, and say,
see how far we've come.
On other days, when they felt like specks,
aphids sucking a spinach stem,
did the people of Paris think of Haussmann,
drawing twelve avenues in a radius

around Napoleon's Arc:
the firm hand,
the straight edge,
indelible ink.

Things

At Spring Grove the patients have nothing to wear:
every day the same thin smocks, empty pockets,
even the tables by their beds are bare.
When it gets too cold, they're stuck inside, they pace
or push themselves against glass doors or metal shelves.

My mother remembers Meissen and silver, Bessarabian rugs,
mahogany chairs, currant and gooseberry bushes.
My grandfather saw his own wife's clothes
on a Russian woman's back in church.
My mother took underwear and sweaters when she fled.

I pass evictions piled onto the curb: beds and dressers,
dark green bags . . . of trash? Whoever's things they are
sleeps somewhere; they stand there in the rain for days.
The Swiss lace collar on my blue silk dress,
the fine edge of bone china on my lip.

Sometimes, heartless, I hand back what my mother gives:
a towel rack, a linen skirt, a bright red belt,
the legacy of years in someone's barn, not knowing
where her father was or if he lived.
That's her life, one of loss and repossession.

Not unlike our friend Anne, whose seven bedrooms brim
with string and rubber bands. Her Armenian father
came here steerage, with only his hands.
She saves wax paper from cereal boxes, labels her art
by price, thinking of her heirs.

Ink bottles, dust jackets, emery boards: ephemera:
come and gone in a day, like lilies, like weather.
It takes a hundred years to make them dear.

All day the tulips' palest lilac pink lingers
like Mozart even when I've left the room.

I used to know a man who owned almost nothing—
a cot, a chair, a chipped glass. I thought
he rose out of bed each morning and floated
free of the sheets, wearing clothes like accidents,
living his life elsewhere.

Everywhere the ghosts of things move in;
the brain mends and polishes their luminous forms.
Sometimes they blurt their way to the tongue.
Mostly they swirl, banging against the gold
in our teeth and the bone of our skulls.

Agoraphobia

Without even trying I can think of a half-dozen women
afraid to drive, including my mother.
Oh, maybe not afraid, period, but afraid of:
highways, the big city, cross country, the beltway,
the high-speed merge, the GW bridge, the circles in D.C.
I always knew it as something to be feared and fought
because it crawls up on you like an ant,
then imbeds itself like a tick that you have to burn out,
pluck by the pincers and shake loose.
But the trick is finding it, figuring out
where it comes from and how it starts: the illness
that keeps you inside for a few weeks,
burgeoning traffic or even some small incident
barely worth mentioning or hardly noticed:
a flat tire, a misplaced key.
I remember my hands trembling on the steering wheel
of my first car, driving around the block,
a new license securely in my purse,
and realizing it was no good, that square of paper.
As I grew older I became conscious of it
in other women, and saw that it wasn't just driving,
that driving was only one facet of this stone:
the friend who stayed in after the birth of her second baby
as if suddenly the door had been locked from the inside,
and she and her daughter were drenched in gasoline
and the world were a burning match.
London shrank to the size of her house.
After a year she made her way to the doctor, the supermarket,
but she'd never really seen the city, and
after a week I knew it better than she
and became her guide. In busses she chattered,

not looking where she was going.
Is the fear more common in beautiful places?
To know that always beyond one's reach is the Place des Vosges
or the Pantheon, to be savored in tandem if at all.
Some women never get over it.
Their worlds shrink to the size of their bodies
and then still smaller, as when they feel their stomachs
wrench at the sound of steps on the street.
This madness carries itself sanely through the hours
as one learns to compensate: having groceries delivered,
living through the telephone.
Like Marlene Dietrich at the end of her life
in a Paris apartment, the feathered boas and smoking jackets
sold discreetly piece by piece to pay for rent.
Fear of the marketplace. Fear of buying and selling
and of oneself being sold,
for when all the clothes and memorabilia were gone,
Dietrich knew that her body—
the legs once insured by Lloyds,
the gravelly voice,
the arched eyebrows—
would be next to go.

The Postcard

Pink tube top with one tit popping out,
eyes rolling like pinballs before they drop,
hair like unbleached flour.
She's shaky on her heels; her body weaves
across the road, a sailboat in a gale,

a mirage of water on a hot street.

I'm not the only one watching:
in my rearview mirror, a pickup truck,
three men, slapping the dashboard with their palms,
hooting like owls.

Thin skin's no jacket to nakedness.

Tomatoes slip their skins so easily when blanched.
Half a minute in boiling water
and the film comes off, in one piece,
like plastic torn from a roll.

She's a red spot on the seat of a white dress,
a splinter in an index finger,
a cigarette tossed out of a car window,
a postcard begging to be read:

Wish you were here
Wish I were there
Wish I were
Wish

The Letter

In Meshed, holy city, beautiful city,
the women wear chadors, holding the long folds
of black cloth closed under their chins,
holding the cloth like the beach holds waves,
holding the cloth closed
with their teeth if their hands carry
a baby, a packet of plums.

Black net even on her face, a woman in Meshed
moves like a phantom across the street,
a letter sealed,
dark rain bleeding the ink of its address.

Dress Code

Adriana tells me I dress "prissy," too neat, too
matched, the colors complementary, the shoes
expensive, Italian, always leather;
not much jewelry and all of it real.
Even as a teenager who succumbed to platform shoes
and bell bottoms, I stopped short
of beads and tie-dye. My mother frowned
at frayed edges and pinned hems, loud
colors and tight skirts: "proletarian,"
she'd sigh, her own clothes like mine
today: in order, tasteful, discreet. They make me
envy a friend who's never had to work
for a living; she carries a plastic purse—
in lime green—and sports black sandals
with brown socks in winter.
Sometimes I wrap scarves and pin jewelry
in odd places, but even when I try
to look bohemian or chic, I still come off
like a page from a mail order catalog, yoked
to double sewn seams and heavy gray wool.
Not even France could change the way I dress.
I think of the Countess de Ribes's
bon mot: "only the bourgeois need real jewels."
My skin's that of a middle manager's
daughter, whose family toiled
its way up the ladder: slipping
down is just a spot of grease away.

A Male in the Women's Locker Room

is a shoe in the refrigerator,
a mouse in the oven. Five years old,
already a *y* chromosome. No, that's not fair,

I don't know that he's a boy
from the bare chest, short hair—
s/he could be her mother's experiment,

like Hemingway. One doesn't have to be a boy
to shoot lions, shirtless, lean with cool aplomb
against the jeep. But how else could he have learned

to kick the stall door hiding his mother,
to move through space as if he owned it,
his solid body absorbing molecules of oxygen

like m&m's. With his pudgy baby hands,
his skin like talcum, he's too young
for an Adam's apple, though his neck

shows promise. Of what? Not ice dancing.
Maybe it's not that he's male but that he's clothed
in navy trunks and I'm just about

to pull off my things. I could go to a stall,
but he's only five. So I strip.
He doesn't crack a smile—what's it like in those joints

with a cover charge and tips? Now his mother's doing
makeup in the mirror; she doesn't see
the way he's watching me, now stark naked. He peers

across the bench, the scientist dismantling DNA;
I'm a goat in a petting zoo.
He takes in my breasts and pubic hair;

it's all her fault. That's mean, he's only five;
she couldn't park him like a car. But no father
would bring his daughter to look

at naked men. If this were Europe, would I care?
The Pilgrims carried modesty like syphilis;
in Sweden he'd have seen so many naked women,

I doubt he'd stare. At three, he'd be cute,
like an animal. At least he's not ten, or twenty-one.
Then, I let myself think what I would do:

Reeling

I never learned this:
It spurts out of each squeezed cell,
tugs at my womb like a silk scarf
caught on a rusty nail.
I wish I could look at men and not feel
my ovaries fall to earth like lady apples,
a short distance, a straight line.
Sometimes it's a smell of soap and smoke
that makes me want to burrow
behind their ears.
Sometimes it's all I can do not to
brush a finger across the mouths
of the boys in my class,
grip their thighs until they jump.
I like to think of them
taking off their jeans
or rummaging through a chest
of underwear to find a comfortable pair.
I'd clap a hand over their eyes,
suck their breath,
hiss, *just do it.*
And it's men with gray hair.
The electrician and his metal box of tools,
blue eyes crisp as frost on a pond
while underneath fish still swim,
the vet with his hands on my cat.
Or even a man who holds himself
closed like a new acorn,
guards each smile like the deed to a house.
If I were Hecate I'd fill
his ruled lines with scribble,

teach him how to talk and chew
at the same time. I'd give him broader palms,
lips less like my father's, who always
bit them, as if reeling in a heavy bass.
Instead, I wear a collar
like a dog patrolling its property,
invisibly fenced,
wired with current.

In College, Linda

was perfect, but for the teeth
she would not let them pull.
Her crowded smile drew
admirers from across lecture halls,
stopped conversations in corridors.
Linda watched her weight and worked her tan—
the rest of us ballooned and paled.
With the discipline of great souls
she could take a bowl of ice cream,
throw half away.
She'd purr into the phone
and roll her eyes, scheduling dates
in shifts, three every Saturday:
drinks, dinner, movie.
We'd roll around in some freshman's
smelly dorm bed while the roommate
cleared his throat outside.
Not Linda. Her dates spent money,
not to mention time.
Eric—A.B.D. in chemistry—would stop
to joke and eat my saltwater taffy,
then escort Linda for coq au vin.
Carson would double park his Mercedes,
listening to Brahms so loud
we could hum along.
If only they had asked us:
we knew Linda didn't like to
touch her underwear. Oh Linda,
not dumb and so pretty
it made your teeth hurt.

Psychosynthesis

You remember your father's breath:
he spits the words; then your mother pops
up, gripping a bucket of bleach,
moaning, "dirt, dirt."
Then you're in first grade standing
in the corner for lying. Later, you ask,
"Am I a liar or was that teacher a bitch?"
From these remnants a body is suspended
over the examination table—paper and drapery
sewn into its skin.
Did it ever breathe? Of course,
it panted like a Chihuahua,
raised in the synapses between nerve endings.
It went to school on the tips of your fingers.
It never did homework.
It gorged on chocolate and capers, sucked epinephrine
from your blood. It grew
into a great poisonous poinsettia,
red and green with leaves the size of a man's foot.
Now it batters the air like egg beaters,
makes the windows rattle,
and you hunch down into the chair
to get away from it.

What Difference Does It Make?

When the giant panda views another
of her species through a window, in a mirror,
does she feel a little less lonely?
I smile when I see another couple like us,
though of course they aren't like us,
except for the contrast
between white skin and black.

The year I turned twelve
the way we live was still a crime;
then *Loving v. Virginia* made race irrelevant
in marriage, told Richard and Mildred they could live
where they were born.

I thought it nothing to write about,
only one kind of difference in a world of difference,
no shame and nothing to brandish like a badge.
I thought that what should not matter, did not.

Others see an *odd couple,*
all she could get, a trophy, a burden.
Has he bought my whiteness with his maleness?
Or does his blackness accompany my womanhood
in the same swampy place?

Through his eyes I see the pain
of interviews that go well on the phone,
the equivocal compliments, followed by *for a . . .*
But I can choose not to see it at all,
as my white skin carries me like a sail.

If you flayed us, you'd notice only the sex,

but it's impossible to live without skin.

Whenever I blurt the word "racist,"
I want to retrieve it, as when
I called a child, "illegitimate";
that night my husband asked,
"What difference does it make?"

Epithets are helicopters
with swords for blades,
but also methods of transport
from here to there.

What our families didn't say and do
was not kind, and then we grew through it like a tree
whose roots invade sewer lines.
Good things—eating, learning, love—
demand openings, penetration,
marriage.
To let the other in,
to not say, *not us.*

Miss Cotton

survived a bus wreck where everyone else died.
She also cured her mother of cancer,
gave herself a tracheotomy,
lifted a car off a boy's leg.

Fiftyish and looming
in large knit suits and oxfords,
she smelled of camphor,
and powder, too dark for her skin.

I sat in the bad row, one of those
who talked during lessons, passed notes in pens.
She told me I was the kind
who needed beating to obey.

My punishments were limited
to afternoons alone with her
describing the taste of cow's blood,
her cousin's amputated feet.

She comes to mind at the supermarket,
and when I stand in front of fourth graders.
Then she rushes through me like a train,
and I want to tell a truth so slant

it makes the soft hair on their bodies
rise and wave,
makes them know
that when the sky is falling,

they can stretch their arms to greet it
and not be crushed.

Tongues

Health class: a diagramed human tongue overhead-
projected two hundred times its normal size.
Taste receptors coded: bitter—back; salt—edges;
sour—sides; and at the tip, sweet.
When I test the hypotheses, flavors melt like soup.
Evenings parked with Gary Weaver, the gearshift in the way:
movies tell us we're supposed to enjoy entwining.

Those who mocked God could lose their tongues.
In 1656, James Nayler, a Quaker, was whipped, branded, and
imprisoned, his tongue cut out.
Denied the wafer chewed until sugar,
he could have still lived a long time
on liquids and gruel, gnawing fruit
between his teeth like horses, gurgling like wells.

Tereus raped Philomela and cut out her tongue,
but she wove a cape that told the story,
the voice of the shuttle, Sophocles called it.
But that's only half: her sister saw the cape and understood.
Some stories float; others are held under
until someone sees a small series of bubbles and knows
there's a body to be dredged.

Quiet students avert their eyes when I ask questions.
The moment I call on someone else,
they look up, bright and intense.
Ambivalence covers them like zebra skin.
I also learned to wait, careful not to offend or usurp.
Sometimes I held my tongue so long, the moment passed,
burning a groove in my mouth.

I like to run my tongue
along another body: from feet to eyelids,
using my organ erect as a knife blade,
causing shivers and pleas to stop.
Gypsies kill men by licking their feet,
making them laugh so much
they asphyxiate.

I have a friend who will eat anything—
kidneys, brains, lungs, heart.
Anything but tongue.
She says it's too, too, too . . .
and can't find the words
for what it is.

II. Summer

Summer

I steep
in its cauldron.
These are days not swallowed
before they breathe.
Their evenings bridge
toward morning, one motion,
a splendid indolence,
a long novel.
This season's not
bound in batting;
it thunders
through thin linen.
I am a slow cooking roast;
by the end of August
my center will be warm
but still red.

Spring Rolls

Cecile, Saigon doctor's daughter, wanted
to elope with her dashing foreign suitor.
Her father made them stay six months
so Cecile could learn to cook,
her fiancé learn to wait.
In '64 he took her home to Germany
where she cleaned her house herself,
perfected what the family cook had taught her,
traveling to Paris each month
for lemon grass, rice paper, *nuoc mam.*
Years later I watched her cook spring rolls
fried crisp and light;
pork pounded thin, garlic-grilled;
cabbage and carrot and cucumber salad.
Like a garden: all balance and contrast:
hot spice relieved by cool crunch;
soft bite of rice vinegar against
tidy texture of rice vermicelli.
I never thought I couldn't go back,
she said, her voice like almond oil.
Why were Americans so half-hearted . . .
She looked at me and then away.
Father died five years ago,
someone in Paris said. My letters go
unanswered, but my packages don't come back,
she went on, waiting
for me to help myself to more.

Appetites

Dein Zug kennt keinen Bahnhof,
my mother would tell me,
astonished at how much
I could consume of whatever
pleased me: ice cream or chocolates,
and later, smoked salmon, Westphalian ham.
Your train knows no station.
Now that I'm an adult, my train knows
several stations, though sometimes
it's a greed express, ripping through
an entire apple tart,
a quart of blueberries,
a pound of Camembert.
All children are greedy
until they learn to curb unattractive habits,
like chewing fingernails or picking noses.
From Old English, *graedig:* Beowulf didn't worry
about how he looked chowing down
a leg of ox or a few pheasants, whole.
A friend taps his wife's frail wrist: *honey,*
wouldn't sorbet be better than ice cream?
Some trains idle and weeds then grow between their tracks.
Once for two weeks I ate nothing,
drinking only mineral water.
I imagined myself light as an airmail letter;
a man's hands could encircle my waist.
I climbed flights of stairs one at a time,
panting. The memory makes me see myself
stare at the shape of a woman
who swims in my pool: her thighs

have the heft of a good dictionary.
She's never sick,
she can lift a lawn mower over the hedge,
she's the only conductor on her train,
and she knows which stations
are worth stopping for.

Leningrad

I've heard stories about hunger:
my mother begging for turnips for two years,
my father roasting the tongues
of his boots when the war ended.
But neither had it as bad as the people
in Leningrad, sieged for nine hundred days, three winters
without food. They traded diamond rings
and icons for meat patties. Human meat,
slightly sweet like horseflesh, though fattier.
I know it's easy to lose one's hunger:
after days, it deepens to a dull ache,
and after weeks of eating nothing,
the body's used itself
for fuel, and food's as foreign as plastic.
But when instead of fasting you eat a little,
you remain ravenous, conscious
of sour breath and the stomach as an open sore,
and eager to admit that everything feeds
on something in this world.
For that admission, nothing expiates, not
the weekly air lift, not
parks lined by avenues of birches, not
voices in candlelit chapels,
and not summers
bathed in long, milky, northern light.

Mussels

Common as mud,
they bubble up everywhere,
breathe through sand,
attach themselves to rocks or seaweed
in great bunches like grapes.
Choose them as you would green beans:
small and light—bigger might be full of silt.
Blue-black, faintly iridescent, bearded
like irises, they smell like the sea,
cooking. Lift the pot and within minutes
they've opened, given up
their savory brine.
Pull out the morsel, not muscle,
much softer, like frog's belly or marshmallow.
Sometimes, nestling in the creamy flesh,
there's a tiny gray pearl, too
small to be prized, a reminder
that values hinge
on contingencies,
and we must be taught
to weigh them.

Salsify

Ugly and inedible root, a witch's finger
pressing hard against a pulse.
Who discovered that peeled and steamed,
it tastes of oysters?

Picture the first bite into a kiwi,
its hairy, brown exterior like a clump of dirt.
Inside: the color of green parrot—shot
with seeds black as pupils.

Or sheep's cheese mottled with mold, an old woman's
arm, salvaged by calling it Roquefort.
A dried ear of corn falls into the fire—
kernels burst like cauliflower, boxer's ears.

Pale as mannequins, calves' feet boiled all day
can make a sparkling jelly. And the ordinary
hen's egg: who would presume it
could produce meringues and mayonnaise?

Cashew pods poison as do
the stems and seeds of mayapples.
Once everything was as wild as
fiddlehead ferns and sharks.

With whisks and knives and flames we stand,
like Custer or Cortez, and tug
our tools through matted pelt:
a shriek, a crack, a welt.

"Game"

refers to the hunters' pleasure,
their season in fresh air
wearing red caps and warm clothes.
The sport takes skill
and the animals that grace it die
a useful death. Along sight lines
the hunters aim clean shots
at pheasant, quail, geese. At home
the birds are plucked and singed,
roasted with juniper,
served with something sour, something sweet:
cranberries or apricots, perhaps,
for the meat is highly flavored.
When you eat it
you must chew gently,
for the buckshot can never be removed;
it becomes part of the bird, like bones,
to be gnawed around, and respected.

Consommé

A heap of bones and flesh,
a root or two: onion stuck with cloves,
celery and water simmered for hours
until the parts give up the right
to be themselves, like citizens
from diverse corners of a country
who sweep across barricades
over the steps of the palace,
and begin to chant.

The king hears the mob banging on the door
but is not sure how to appease them.
The soup is strong,
but muddy, clotted with debris.
For consommé, it must be chilled,
boiled again with fresh meat, and sieved.
Then it's flesh made liquid,
sparkling clear like a mountain lake
you can see a body through.

Eating Crabs with Bob and Jim

Hammering and cracking, shards of shell flying,
clothes coated with juice and spice—
I love picking carelessly,
knowing the crabs won't run out.
My friends enjoy their labors differently:
Jim's from New Orleans so his finesse shows
in the way he flips the tab on males,
opens them briskly, coaxes out jumbo lump.
Bob operates like an orthopedist,
clears debris at regular intervals,
focuses on one claw at a time.
He's not been well, so he's taking it slow.
Anyway, there we are sucking sweet meat
from cartilage, swilling beer, and suddenly Bob says,
"Damn, I've cut myself. Do you have a Band-Aid?"
We both jump up and I look
at his hand, only a scratch, but bleeding.
I can feel my wheels turn—
information comes two ways, says Jung:
through our senses or our intuition.
Though of course it doesn't matter
how I registered a difference
in the way he jumped up
and the way I did, the way
someone would to whom a drop of blood
is just a drop of blood.

A Short History of the Sybarites

—600 B.C.
The Sybarites sleep in silver
beds, on mattresses stuffed with sponges.
They rise at noon, steam bathe, work
their slaves. Some train
horses to dance to flutes;
others play with Maltese puppies,
dye their hair.

—575 B.C.
The Sybarites catch snails
roused from winter's sleep. Their bodies curl
and stretch—best and most tender then, the ravenous
mollusks feast on grape leaves.
Then they're soaked, washed, blanched,
pulled from the shell and gutted.

—550 B.C.
The Sybarites master the banquet arts.
Cooks compete with specialties: turtle doves
tucked inside roast partridge;
oysters and scallops under puréed peas;
fat snails, simmered four hours in herbs
and wine. Each guest is given
a golden spear to skewer his snails,
takes it home as a souvenir.

—530 B.C.
The Sybarites forget how to write,
though one boy takes an interest in a pen;
considers paper, painted, to decorate the walls.
Hippolochus sends a letter home:

These people wave away tomorrows
like mosquitos from the plain.
However, I'm certainly eating well.

     —510 B.C.

Seventy miles south, the Crotons
plot to conquer Sybaris. They learn
the tune their enemies' horses dance to.
In battle the Sybarites' steeds frolic
instead of charge;
their city's razed and burned.

     —410 B.C.

A woman scrubs the steps of a Croton house.
Sometimes after rain, snails come out;
they inch across her path.
She could crack their shells with a stone,
expose soft pulsing heads.
Instead she leans back,
and her sigh escapes
like notes from a flute.

What I Want to Make for You

First I'll find two pears,
green speckled with yellow,
the color of locust trees in May,
two specimens that yield
to slight pressure from my thumb.
They'll sit in the sun, next to an apple
whose ethylene breath will ripen them more,
to the point where even the faintest touch
would bruise them. Then I'll spread out
several leaves of phyllo, sweet
buttering each one with a sable brush,
between whose sheets I'll slip
toasted, slivered, blanched almonds.
I'll cut the pastry into hearts,
one for each of us, baking until crisp—
not long—in the hot oven waiting.
You haven't forgotten the pears?
My knife is so sharp it won't hurt
when I peel and slice them.
More sweet butter and sugar sizzle
in a pan, plus heavy cream,
unctuous, languid, sleepy,
and the pears with some eau de vie,
then a rapid simmer.
Now the assemblage:
One nutty heart on the bottom,
soft sautéed pears in the middle,
another fragile heart on top.
A pool of glossy caramel cream,
also on my fingers with which I offer you
ce mille feuille croquant de poire
au caramel.

Chocolates

My mother taught me how to prize them:
on the couch, my father gone to bed,
watching Audrey Hepburn, Deborah Kerr
choose among suitors, decide what to wear.
We'd allocate and savor: marzipan and Cointreau,
mocha truffle and praline, soft
cinnamon cream covered with crisp dark crunch.

I learned to discriminate sweet
sludge, generic, from the known and European:
Rumpelmayer, Neuhaus, Lindt, Perugina.
Later, too old for easy endings,
we'd demand more than our share,
sting each other to tears,
mouths closed as though we'd swallowed bees.

Like cuckoo clocks and racing cars
chocolates require precision,
but like capers or caviar
they must be consumed before they bloom
or break. And then they dissolve
to nothing on the tongue, like names
called out in anger, and in love.

Rampion

Let us praise this most polynomial
of plants: In English it's lamb's lettuce,
named perhaps for the delicate ear
or tonguelike leaves.
Imagine a small cat's paw
or a spoon for demitasse.
We also call it corn salad,
growing as it does protected
from the sun between stalks.
The French say *mâche*
but also *blanchette* (little white)
clairette (little light)
doucette (little soft)
oreillette (little ear).
In Latin, it's *valerian,*
akin to catnip, the bellflower
whose medicinal roots prevent spasms.
One pays dearly for this plant
because it's hard to clean, demanding
a large tub of cool water and someone
to lift it slowly
many times, spurning
the grass and grains of sand.
But worth the trouble for its leaves smooth
as mayonnaise, colored
like clover, flavored of walnuts.
To some it's salad, to others
it's a fairy tale. The stuff
Rapunzel's mother craved

and that the old witch grew and guarded.
The stuff an unborn child is bartered for.
It recalls the persistence of desire.

III.

Red Under the Skin

Seeing is forgetting the name of the thing one sees.
—Paul Valéry

The hatred goes back for centuries, everyone says,
    a tradition as old
        as making wine, weaving rugs, playing flutes.

My father remarks
    he would have expected it
from the Croats
      who colluded with Hitler,
    but not the loyal Serbs.

      Being Slovene makes him proud:
  efficient factories, clean streets, their own language,
        independence.

     Forty years of exile, and he goes back
       and is proud.

          He never lost his accent.

When people ask me what I am,
    my friend Aida says, *what am I to say?*

Serbian Orthodox father.
Bosnian Muslim mother.
Croatian Catholic husband.

    I used to call myself a Serb.
It was healing, you see, through intermarriage and friendship.
It WAS healing.

It was.

Now, nothing
she can do six thousand miles away.
Or even there, what difference would it make?

One more death, like the husband of her best friend
who couldn't believe it, who walked out into the streets
of Sarajevo disbelieving, who was felled
by the first sniper bullets. Who cared
that he was a Serb married to a Muslim,
who had left Belgrade for love?

                                    Friends are cutting
her off, Aida says, because her family isn't *pure*.

Americans of Serbian or Croatian descent. Not recent emigrants,

        but those like my father, who have been here for years.

It starts with rallies,
as in Belgrade in the fall of '88,
with Serbs chanting:

        We are the victims of

        The world is trying to extinguish

        We will fight until

Like campaign buttons
            or bumper stickers. Nothing to be ashamed of
                    letting the neighbors hear.
                    Who was listening?

In the Serb-Croatian War of 1991 (that war?
        war
                and more war)

the fiercest fighters were the émigrés,
        Croatians who returned
                from Canada or Australia or Germany
                   or the U.S.

      to a land they knew only in the stories

of their parents.

          What were they told?

What the papers don't tell:
      Muslim, Orthodox, Catholic, Jew
          put up Christmas trees, exchanged gifts.

The Baptist on the plane asks me what denomination I am.

      His salary's tithed to Oral Roberts;
          his daughter has married a Palestinian
             whose fervor he can understand.

Nothing, I tell him, I'm not Christian.

What then, he asks, an edge in his voice, *are you Buddhist?*
      Muslim?

      And then,
I only want to save you from eternal damnation.

          Denomination.
          Domination.
       To name and to classify.
       To know by looking,
       and through naming.

To walk in the forest
and say, *Arisaema triphyllum,*
                    jack-in-the-pulpit,
                              Hypericum punctatum,
                                        spotted Saint-John's-wort.

Or *Boletus luridus*
              (poisonous).

              How to see?
How to speak without naming,
                    without letting the name blind us,
                              without letting the name speak
                                        by itself.

How will people know me if I write,
                                        Natasha Sajé,
                              white,
                    American,
              born in *Munich,*
                    Silesian mother,
                          Slovene father,
                                Catholics.

              But wasn't there a Polish great-great-grandfather

and a Jew

                    somewhere on my mother's side?

              We Americans don't understand it,

                          defining difference as we do by looking.

You don't look Indian.
You don't look Jewish.
You don't look black.

When we're all the same shade of brown,

      when our bodies have ground out their differences

          through eons of intermarriage,

            when we speak the same language,

             when . . .

Then they look the same as you, the Muslims,

        how can you tell what they are if they look the same?

Well, there's always the name.

Mine's a riddle.

            In Slovene "saje" means soot.

In villages and cities where carbon
             coats the buildings
                and one's skin
           with the finest layer of black grit—
you get used to it—
          you wipe a finger across your cheek
             and then there's a black
               smudge on your white shirt.

Did they wear dark shirts
     because they couldn't rid themselves
                      of dust?

My mother disapproved of Girl Scouts,
     smacks of Hitler Youth, she said.

I must have had a German accent once
        because children called me Hitler's daughter.
    I told them where I was born; I liked
        being different.

My godfather was in Dachau
        where they put straw under his nails
                until it stuck in the pink flesh
                    and then they lit it.

One day he was told he'd be killed
    tomorrow
                and the next day
                    the Americans liberated the camp.

He's a Catholic priest who's spent
            his life in Germany,
                who won't go back to Slovenia
                    until every last Communist is dead,
                        he says.

        We Americans say, *I'm half Polish and half Italian* or

I'm part Scotch and part Irish.

            In the old country, we buy
souvenirs, trace the headstones of our ancestors
        with a reverent finger, feel
                    the hills and rivers as part of us.

        What part?

The part longing for a home

                        the part lost

when people scattered

from villages and drifted to cities,

the part that mourns.

Telling who is good from who is bad is not so easy anymore.

On election day a young man hands me a pamphlet:

Jews are running this country;
blacks are ruining it.
Do you want to be turned out
of your own country?

From Latin, *contra,* against,

the land lying opposite

or before one.

We are each other's country,

we are each other's marrow:

to be sucked for sustenance,

depleted by disease,

or to grow

richer

and redder

and darker.

IV. Body Language

Water Music

Once her wide net could catch all kinds of fish
all day and all night:
soft and fleshy weaks; triggers, fast-finned;
hard-spiked urchins and walleyed pikes;
and stentor; plankton; orange krill.
She was never hungry, and after a while
the stuff made wallpaper, postcards, pumice stones.

Then she learned how unladylike it looked,
that huge stinking thing trailing behind,
and she wanted to rip it apart,
but its skeins were stronger than silk,
so she became fastidious instead,
throwing stuff back and thinking,
not this one, not that one;
saying, *sorry, sorry.*

When they stained her clothes she threw them away.
When they looked at her funny she threw them away.
When she was afraid she'd be caught she threw them away.

She spent most of her time throwing.

That lasted a long while,
half the life of a peach tree,
the entire life of the average house cat.
Her arms grew so tired she couldn't swim,
and she found herself beached,
the net draped around her like a bridal gown.
The only thing she could do was read the dictionary,
which she used like a phone book,
calling up each word and waiting

to hear a voice on the other side,
hello, hello.

The words hung up as soon as they heard her.

One day in the *p*'s, between *plagal*—
a medieval mode with a range from the fourth below
to the fifth above—and *plague*—
till the seven plagues of the seven angels were fulfilled—
she found *plagiarism,* from Latin for kidnap,
from *plaga* for net.
Knowing what to call it was such an immense relief,
she fairly hummed with happiness,
specifically Handel's *Water Music,*
to which she added the lyrics,
mea culpa, mea culpa.
She'd just have to learn to fish so well
people would admire her for it,
saying, oh, what a big fine net you have,
and oh, what a deep briny smell.

Edith Wharton After the Death of Henry James

Whenever I write a story, Henry,
I feel your bulk behind me,
blocking the cold air,
casting a shadow on the page.
Sometimes you "hrmph"
when I let a chance slip,
or you pinch my hand
to make me take out commas.
Mostly you tap your foot,
amused at my efforts,
knowing the end before I do.
Today you droned, "Invoke your demon of patience,"
and I realized you'd never said a word before.
Did you think I had forgotten you?
Was letting you slip off
like a wedding band from a thin finger?
Or did my method seem lax—
you would have worn a cravat,
sat upright at a desk
or paced the room like an expectant father,
your baritone a scalpel carving syllables.
Did you spy me reclining
on the divan in my robe,
a bowl of white roses on the table,
the window open to luscious green hills?

L'Oustau de Baumanière

—Les Baux de Provence

An occasional motor hums in the distance.
But mostly the wings of moths
against glass, murmured conversation.
A scent of pipes and lavender.
I think this inn was a convent once—
three hundred years ago to these low vaults women fled
or were ditched, daughters without dowries
who learned to savor the taste of coarse bread.
In black-and-white gowns they made their rounds,
watched the world of men dissolve like soap.
On stone floors, our oak chairs rest like thrones.
The waiters wear soft soles, bring
asparagus cut this morning from stalks planted long ago;
and *mousserons:* trumpet mushrooms small
as infant fingers, gathered from the forest's secret patches.
Today we stood on the village peak—
an eagle's nest, Richelieu said, before he razed it.
Tonight the azure sea's red mullet swims in *pistou*
made with basil from the garden
and oil from olive trees a few miles south.
The silver feels like pistols in our hands.
We talk in metaphor: I'm red pumps,
you're a tortoise comb,
together we're an undiscovered planet's largest star.
I feel your mind span a bridge
through our shared past.
Through pine-nut cake, thyme and honey ice cream.
If we were indigenous here, like scrub brush
or bauxite, they'd have to pull us apart

by the roots or mine us with machines.
Our voyage grafts us, a sort of honeymoon:
two women spend a lot of money on a meal
they'll never forget.
A hundred years ago I would be writing:
Dear Laura,
Let us travel together again,
to this place where our voices sing
from within walls three feet thick.
Where we draw sustenance from one another,
like water taken, on a warm day in June,
from deepest wells.

Mountains

Before, when I lived in the mountains,
it was Switzerland, and winter, and I was twenty.
In the noon sun on terraces, people wore bathing suits,
and I brought them coffee and ice cream.
Some shusshed down the slopes, edges cutting ice.
A few climbed and died, losing their footing
or swept under an avalanche of snow.
Each day I went to work and each night
I wept. No one I loved would know
if I died. It would take days for them to find me.

These Sierra mountains are smaller, browner,
striped with straggly pines, with columbine
and wild poppies tumbling from dry grass.
They cup me like a firefly in their hands.
When I go home, someone will be glad to see me,
and we will resume our rituals of morning tea,
of calling each other's names to come to bed;
in between we'll seldom speak. And if
I wish for our lives to be different,
I will inhale that wish like oxygen.

Body Language

When you know the bend of someone's shoulder
better than your own because you have seen it
from every angle for so many years,
when you have learned that body
like a language for which the grammar is imprinted
on the brain in a space reserved
for connections made without thinking, then
only the perspective changes:
remote as an arc of stars,
intimate as a spoon in your mouth.
But though you recognize that body's permutations,
you can't imagine where
they will take you, and part of that freedom
is fear. It's a mistake to lean on any body;
you must be satisfied
not with the thing itself—
frail, vile, glorious—
but with the way you know it.
Your gift is reading that body
in a crowd, at a distance—
its slight dejected turn, ebullient lilt,
or especially the feeling you'll never find
words for, but you know
how to answer anyway.

On a City Street

With a finger he lifts her chin,
then bends his head and kisses her
on the mouth, lightly.

Pleasure washes through me like champagne.
How did he learn to bow so gently lilaclike?
How did she learn to stand so still?

Would I rather be her, waiting in that second
between the finger and the kiss,
or him, enacting the gift?

Or the person gazing at them both,
turning the vanishing moment into words.
This is not a kiss. Dear reader,

what do you feel upon reading of this?
Do the words enter you like blackberries
or someone else's breath?

At twenty, I yearned to meet a lover
on a broad sidewalk in spring,
while a café of people turned their heads

to sigh at our resplendent bliss.
But would I have known what to make of it then,
what to call it or how to savor it?

I might have been thinking only
of my crooked teeth or badly fitting bra.
Since then I've become a connoisseur

of reading, of this couple who stand,
like a hyphenated word,
amid the babble of passersby

on a June afternoon,
the day after my thirty-eighth birthday,
after an evening spent with friends of twenty years

choosing what to tell, and censoring
the rest the obsessions
that stood behind us like columns of fire

at once illuminating and darkening us,
in silhouette.
We spoke easily of what we had,

of what we wanted. Fed, clothed, and sheltered,
we punctuated our desires
for a house in the country,

a transatlantic practice,
a book, with shrugs and understatement.
Some things we know only through the telling;

telling slakes the vacant ache
of wishing for something that never happened,
of waiting for Gary Cooper or King Kong

to appear at the door,
hands out, palms up.
I have unlearned unhappiness

like the habit of biting my nails,
disallowed the small, nervous, chipping away.
How easy it is to be happy: it's enough

to tell a stranger of a wonderful kiss,
a day when light soaks into the skin,
when we can see glimpses of other people's lives

that could belong to us,
that do.

Dental Work

Lying back with the tray table nudging
a shoulder and a square light so bright
I close my eyes and think of England
in June, all yellow mustard fields and pink roses;

but that's the only way to travel, because if I moved,
I'd jar the drill into my cheek.
Turquoise walls and ugly machines make my body
the most interesting thing in the room and

a dentist's finger is the next best thing to food,
though those rubber gloves all taste the same,
faintly of cocoa butter. Food's gotten me
into this spot in the first place, bacteria colonizing

on strawberry twizzlers and maple butter caramels;
now I must wait quietly for the wasp
to break its circuit and buzz away.
At least this is no dream of teeth crumbling

at the first bite of an apple,
turning to powder in my palm,
and no naturalist novel,
with McTeague's enormous wrist yanking

out the wrong incisor, and I'm not Berenice
whose crazy cousin violated her body
for the pearls in her mouth. No, I'm not a victim
here, though my heart is beating very fast,

from the memory of adrenalin, and fear,
and from thinking about these men

leaning over me like weeping willows.
Dear Cyril, dental student from long ago, Cyril

with the green eyes, whose gold onlay in my molar
has an overhang, was I a check
in the appropriate column or did you think of me
the way I am thinking of you now,

tenderly?
Even the ones who make money at it,
who wear expensive watches, I like the way they notice
my pain, stop when I raise an eyebrow

or narrow my lids. I forget that they're crowning
with metal and porcelain the smile
of the waiting skeleton, giving me something stronger
than the bone I was born with.

A Kind of Steamed English Pudding
with Raisins

That's Spotted Dick, the name we give
the cat who haunts our back porch,

who rubs his whiskers on the cedar,
tacking on his scent as though

he had hammer and nails.

If he were a dog, he'd be a Dalmatian;
as a dance he's the polka.

His brothers solid and sleek, tuxedoed;
he's an ocular tickle,

Mussolini's typewriter
or the Brussels suburbs.

But he trots down the avenue
with his tail high and waving,

a royal fern, a whiff of fur.

He's black tulip petals in the snow,
a doubleheaded nickel,

the odd man at a dinner party

who drinks from his neighbor's glass,
spills blueberries on white linen,

but is always asked back.

An aesthetic faux pas
with the charm of things awry:

Rubens's Queen Medici, rolling
from the ship like a barrel;

a choirboy's voice cracking.
He looks astonished when I coo to him,

like he's been caught with a paw in the door.
I look at him and laugh:

pudding head, sweet cake.

Then What Is the Question?

They've computed the planes of her face,
which match his exactly. Leonardo painted
himself as Woman: a horse of spirit

underneath the odd bright dresses.
Love child, who bought caged birds to set them free.
Who wrote and wrote from right to left like Hebrew.

Who asked, *why worship the son when all churches
are dedicated to the mother?* South paw.
To read the writing you need a mirror,

the way you do to see your own face;
to see the back of your head, you need two.
Say cheese: look at the artist's smile

and say cheese. Mona Lisa's an aged Dutch gouda:
a cheese that bites back.
Eat it with beer.

Eat it with pity for simple young brie.
Eat it and figure in a painting: Outside
the landscape's unbroken

flatness won't hide canals and dykes.
Inside, gloves litter a checkered tile floor.
Crisp light streaks through leaded panes.

A clavier awaits a pair of hands:
brazen maiden with androgynous smile,
gay young cavalier in ruffled cuffs and feathered hat.

Walter Pater, did you know Mona as a boy?

Boys will be boys, excused of killing tadpoles
or talking back to mother. Boys as women,

at center stage; women as Hamlet, Peter Pan.
Did Gertrude wish she were a boy? The happiest person
Alice had ever known, who referred to her as "he."

S/he liked the Louvre, but preferred to stay in bed
till noon, walk the dog, and write.
S/he owned a painting by Judith Leyster:

a woman sewing. *She with a sheet of linen.*
He with a sheet of paper. Genders bend
like sheets of rain or wrap like shrouds.

Alice stewed prunes in cinnamon and Rhône wine,
embroidered lingerie; her lover wrote:
You are my honey honey suckle. I am your bee.

Freud traced it all to Leonardo's mother,
the bird of prey who suckled him.
But this bird's a kite, with a tail

that's forked, a tongue telling two stories.
One calls the smile the essence of the feminine,
her deceitful will to seduce.

It carries a ruler on its tip: condemned
to always come up short.
The other is sharp as a boy's trick,

deflating art's high balloon
with a prick. Crashing the party,
declaring it a bore:

Elle a chaud au cul.
Remember the tail, said Freud.
She's got hot pants, she's hot to trot, her tail's hot,

that's not why she's smiling, is it?
To burn always with this hard, gemlike flame.
Tradition's a prison, groaned Duchamp, in drag:

RRose Sélavy. A million bees make a pound of honey,
and all for one queen. *That's not art,* roared Teddy R.
The mirror's slivered into shards,

the smile's a trace; Alice might have shaved.
Gerty's deathbed words:
Then what is the question?

Natasha Sajé _____

was born in Munich, Germany, in 1955, and grew up in New York City and northern New Jersey. She earned a B.A. from the University of Virginia and an M.A. from Johns Hopkins University, and is currently a Ph.D. candidate at the University of Maryland at College Park, completing a study of the coquette figure in the American novel. Her poems and essays appear in many journals, including *Antaeus, Poetry, Ploughshares,* and *Signs: Journal of Women in Culture and Society.* She has received grants from the Maryland State Arts Council and from the city of Baltimore. *Red Under the Skin* won the 1993 Agnes Lynch Starrett Poetry Prize.

PITT POETRY SERIES

ED OCHESTER, GENERAL EDITOR